# 20TH CENTURY SCIENCE & TECHNOLOGY



# 1990-2000 ELECTRONIC AGE

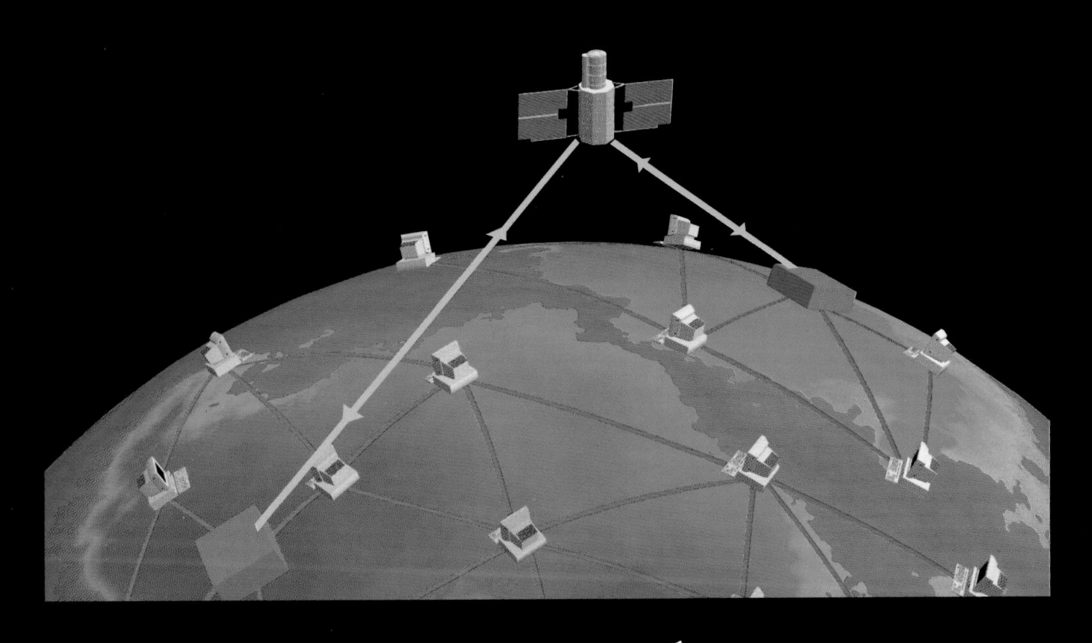

Steve Parker

Heinemann LIBRARY

# CONTENTS

*Space scientists are fairly certain that, apart from Earth, life exists on no other planets in the Solar System. But what about their moons, such as Saturn's Titan?*

*New engineering methods and materials allow skyscrapers, like the Petronas Towers, to grow ever higher.*

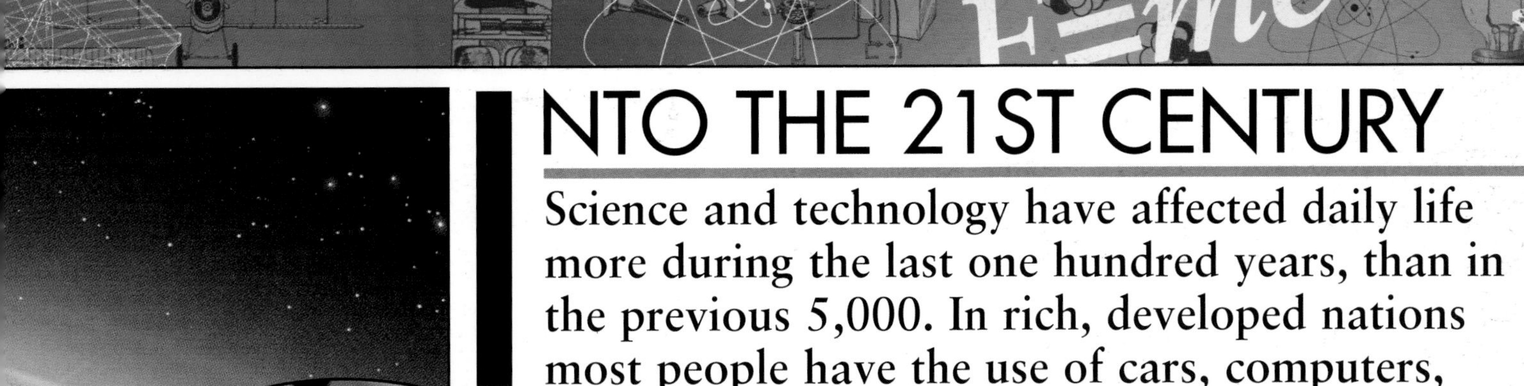

# NTO THE 21ST CENTURY

Science and technology have affected daily life more during the last one hundred years, than in the previous 5,000. In rich, developed nations most people have the use of cars, computers, mobile phones and domestic appliances such as dishwashers. We watch live global TV and gain instant Internet access to the span of human knowledge, almost without a second thought. Yet science is a 'double-edged sword'. It has led to nuclear weapons, global warming, acid rain, smog and other massive pollution problems. Piles of radioactive waste grow and vast areas of natural beauty are destroyed. Despite medicine's success in controlling disease, and agriculture's progress in producing food, one quarter of the world's people are still diseased or hungry. Can we use science and technology more wisely and fairly in the 21st century?

*The wind-up radio combines high-tech electronic circuits with a low-tech clockwork motor.*

*Medical science has unravelled the secrets of human genes, which will hopefully lead to many new treatments and cures.*

*Electric 'eco-cars' consume fewer natural resources when made, use less energy, reduce pollution and occupy less road space.*

*'Electronic pets' became a toy craze in the mid 1990s. They had to be fed and cared for, or they would become ill and die.*

# IS ANYTHING REAL?

**The century began with Einstein's mind-bending ideas on space, time and relativity. It ended with even more amazing notions of infinite universes, time travel, life in cyberspace and the nature of 'reality' itself.**

*Using VR the auto engineer can see, design and build a new engine. But it is only images in the headset, not a physical object.*

## SEEMS REAL, IS UNREAL

Virtual reality, VR, makes an object or scene seem real to our sight, hearing, touch and other senses. But it is not real. It is unreal or virtual. The object or scene does not exist as a physical item. It exists only in the mind as make-believe. The brain builds up an impression of reality from the information fed to the body's senses by computer-controlled devices, such as a headset with earphones to make sounds and small screens showing pictures. The devices 'trick' the senses and brain.

*A medical scientist can move and manipulate this virtual model of a new drug molecule, to test if it is more effective.*

## LIVING IN A VIRTUAL WORLD

VR took off in the '90s as computers advanced to 'real time' processing. This means the computer can analyze huge amounts of incoming information and generate changing sounds, images and movements at the speed we experience in actual life. VR is used to train pilots, firefighters, surgeons and sports people, to design cars, clothes, chemicals and shopping malls, and in countless other ways.

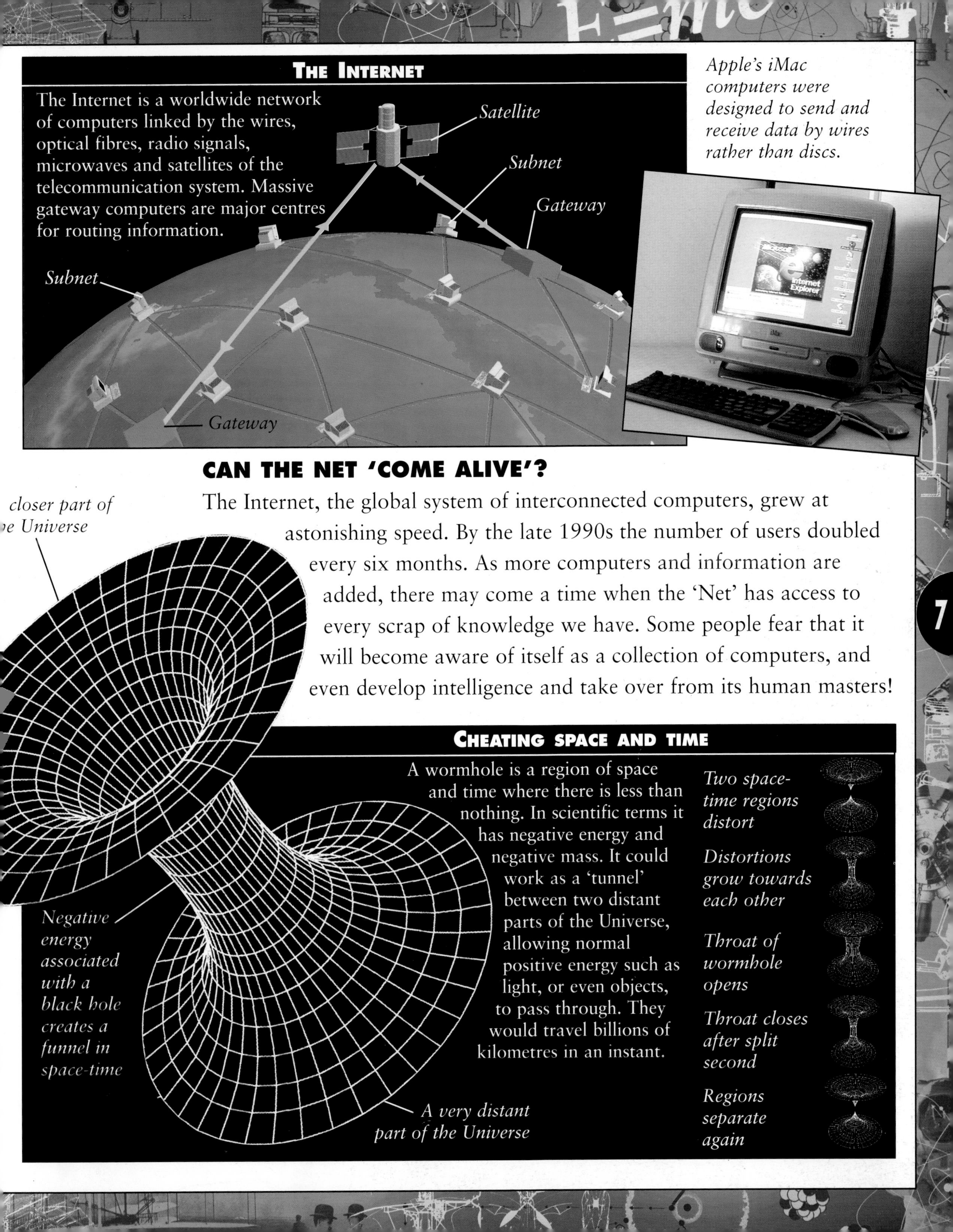

## The Internet

The Internet is a worldwide network of computers linked by the wires, optical fibres, radio signals, microwaves and satellites of the telecommunication system. Massive gateway computers are major centres for routing information.



*Apple's iMac computers were designed to send and receive data by wires rather than discs.*

## CAN THE NET 'COME ALIVE'?

The Internet, the global system of interconnected computers, grew at astonishing speed. By the late 1990s the number of users doubled every six months. As more computers and information are added, there may come a time when the 'Net' has access to every scrap of knowledge we have. Some people fear that it will become aware of itself as a collection of computers, and even develop intelligence and take over from its human masters!

## Cheating space and time

A wormhole is a region of space and time where there is less than nothing. In scientific terms it has negative energy and negative mass. It could work as a 'tunnel' between two distant parts of the Universe, allowing normal positive energy such as light, or even objects, to pass through. They would travel billions of kilometres in an instant.

1990-2000

# SPACE SECRETS

**The 1990s was a mixed time for space science. In particular Mars, the 'Red Planet', grabbed many headlines. Microscopic 'sausages' found in a lump of Martian rock were even hailed as signs of alien life.**

## A NEW VIEW

In 1990 the US launched the Hubble Space Telescope, HST, into orbit around Earth. Far above the hazy, dusty atmosphere, the telescope should have had a clear view into space. However its mirror had not been polished to an accurate curve so the view was blurred. In 1993, space shuttle astronauts fitted 'contact lenses' to correct the problem.

*Space shuttle astronauts fitted more new equipment to the Hubble Space Telescope in 1997. The telescope was held near the main cargo bay, doors wide open. The shuttle's wing tips show on either side.*

*The Hubble Telescope is 13 m long, about the size of a 52-seater bus, and orbits 613 km above Earth's surface. The flap on the right is the aperture door, open to allow in light.*

*Russian space station* Mir, *launched in 1986, suffered several accidents in the 1990s. In June 1997 an unmanned* Progress *craft, ferrying supplies and taking away wastes, bumped into the ageing structure. By 1999* Mir *was 'mothballed' in orbit. But a new, bigger space station was being assembled (see next page).*

### ALIEN SAUSAGES?

In 1984 geologists collected a fist-sized piece of rock from Antarctica as part of a scientific survey. In 1993 it was studied and found to come from Mars, probably blasted from the surface as a large meteorite crashed into the planet. The lump became a tiny meteorite itself for 15 million years and fell to Earth 13,000 years ago. Microscopes revealed tiny sausage-like shapes, each 100 times thinner than a human hair, in the rock. Were these long-preserved remains of Martian microbes? There is no clear answer.

*A piece of Mars with its tube-like 'micro-fossils' (right).*

## MYSTERIOUS MARS

Mars, our nearest planet neighbour, was visited in 1993 by US space probe *Mars Observer*. At least, that was the plan. The probe 'went dead' as radio contact was lost on approach – a costly failure at $9 billion. In 1996, scientists described evidence for possible life on Mars billions of years ago (see panel above). Then in 1997 came brilliant success. The probe *Mars Pathfinder* soft-landed and sent back amazing live TV images as its wheeled, skateboard-sized rover vehicle *Sojourner* trundled across the soft red dust. It moved at one centimetre per second, guided by its own lasers and other sensors, and by an operator here on Earth. Sadly, the year before, the US announced that its manned mission to Mars was delayed, probably until 2020.

*Hubble has taken many awe-inspiring images of deep space, more than 100 times clearer than telescopes on the ground. This is a small part of the Lagoon Nebula, a wispy region where new stars are born and old ones die.*

# TO THE FUTURE

**In 1984, Ronald Reagan, the US President, announced a major new space project – a giant space station code-named 'Freedom'. After many delays and cutbacks, by the mid 1990s it had become the ISS, International Space Station.**

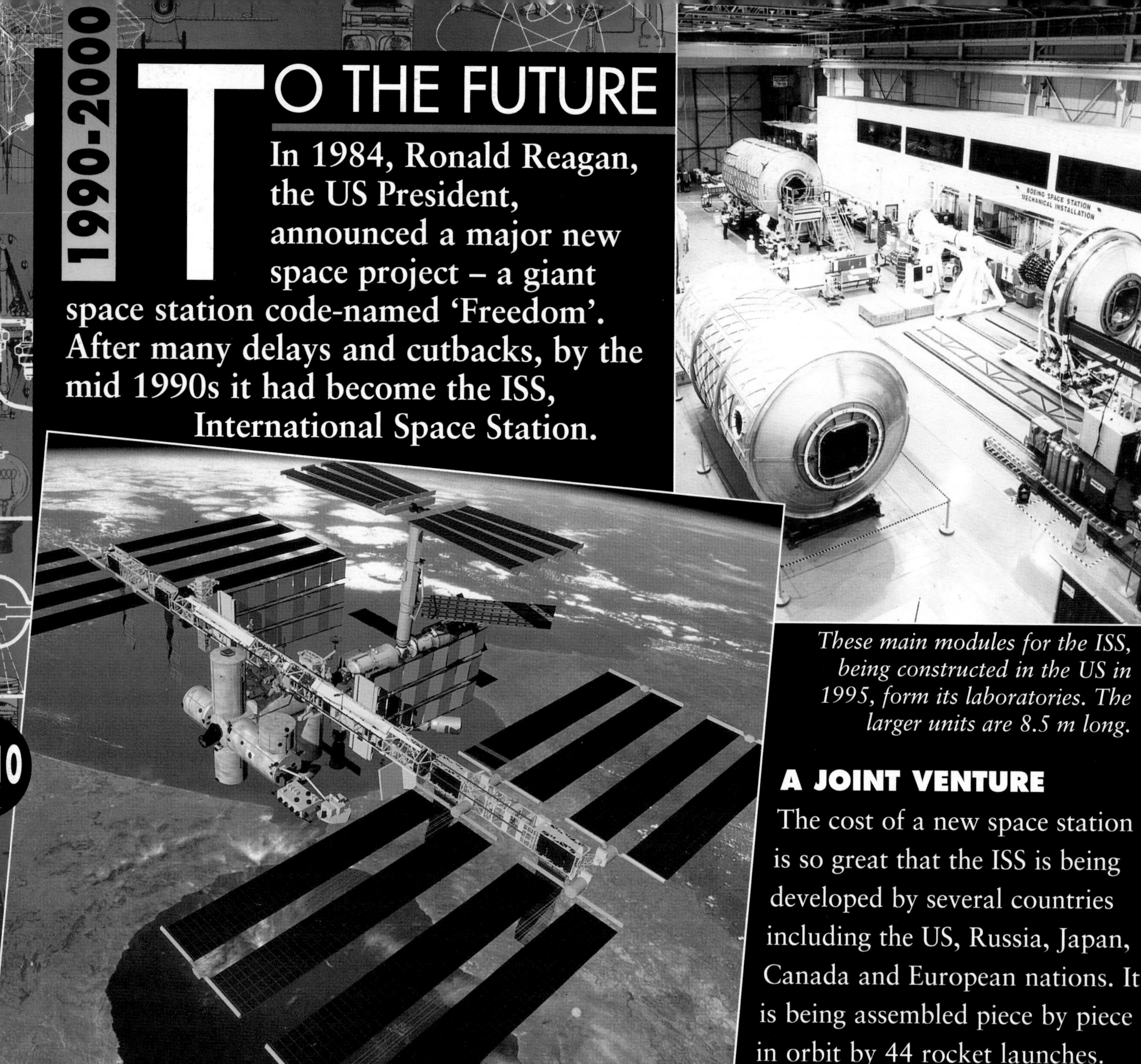


*These main modules for the ISS, being constructed in the US in 1995, form its laboratories. The larger units are 8.5 m long.*

*Artist's impression of the ISS shows vast solar panels which cover the area of a soccer pitch. The station would weigh 400 tonnes on Earth's surface, but in orbit 400 km high it is weightless.*

## A JOINT VENTURE

The cost of a new space station is so great that the ISS is being developed by several countries including the US, Russia, Japan, Canada and European nations. It is being assembled piece by piece in orbit by 44 rocket launches. Original completion date was about 1995, but by the year 2000 this had moved on to 2005.

## WHY ISS?

Why spend billions of dollars on the ISS when ordinary people could benefit from the money? Practical reasons include the lack of gravity, which means super-pure substances can be made in orbit, such as crystals for microchips. New materials and technologies may 'spin off' into daily life. There is also the lure of fantastic new discoveries in deep space that may change our ideas about the origin and fate of the Universe.

## A distant world

*2004: In Saturn orbit, Huygens separates from Cassini.*

On arrival at Saturn, the Cassini-Huygens probe separates. Cassini orbits the planet, studying its rings and atmosphere. It is named after Giovanni Cassini (1625–1712) who discovered four of Saturn's moons and also the gap in its rings now called the Cassini division. Huygens detaches and plunges towards Titan, slowing by parachute to land. It radioes information about the moon's gases and surface to Cassini, which relays it back to Earth. It is named after Christiaan Huygens (1629–95) who discovered Saturn's rings and its moon Titan.

*Lander's atmosphere-entry dish protects craft.*

*Parachute opens at height of 170 km.*

*Lander settles on Titan*

## STILL BOLDLY GOING

The last main unmanned mission of the 1990s was the Cassini-Huygens space probe. After nail-biting delays it set off in 1997 to arrive at the giant outer planet of Saturn in 2004. The Cassini orbiter should circle the planet itself, studying its beautiful rings, while the Huygens lander approaches Saturn's largest moon, Titan. Among all the planets and moons in our Solar System, scientists believe that Titan may once have had conditions suitable for life – at least, life as we know it.

### THE MICRO-ROCKET

Big rocket engines for space travel are hugely expensive, heavy and thirsty for fuel. The micro-rocket is just 3 mm thick and 15 mm wide, and burns methane and oxygen gases as fuel. But weight-for-weight is 20 times more efficient than a big rocket engine. It is estimated that 800 micro-rockets could launch a one-tonne craft into space. Like an electronic microchip, the micro-rocket is made from a wafer of the substance silicon.

*The micro-rocket is smaller than a thumb-tip.*

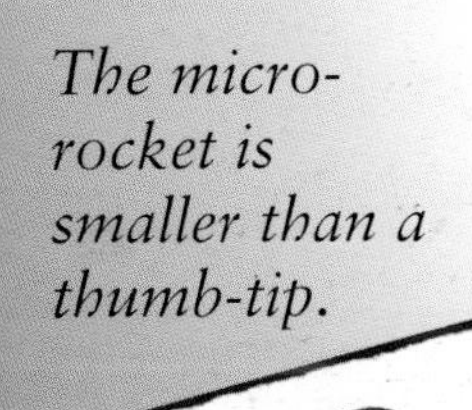

# ON THE MOVE

After the boom of the 1960s and the bust of the '70s-80s, travel and transport settled down in the 1990s (see page 14). But there was still room for being fast, big and expensive.

*A Global Positioning System device allows travellers to know their location to within a few metres* *(see page 21)**.*

*A new type of maglev (magnetic levitation) train tested in Japan in 1997 achieved speeds of about 800 km/h.*

*Japan's ultra-streamlined electric inter-city trains travel as fast as some passenger aircraft.*

## MASS TRANSIT

In Japan a third generation of sleek, fast 'bullet trains' reached speeds of 300 kilometres per hour. These ran on the usual system of wheels and rails, although the railway lines must be very straight and super-smooth. 'Maglev' trains, suggested as far back as the 1930s, were still being explored in the '90s but made little headway. A maglev vehicle floats above the track, held up by the force of magnetic pushing or repulsion.

## Auto-car

Radio signals from satellites and local ground beacons can tell a vehicle its exact position. They might even help the driver to operate the controls so that the car follows the correct route to its pre-programmed destination.

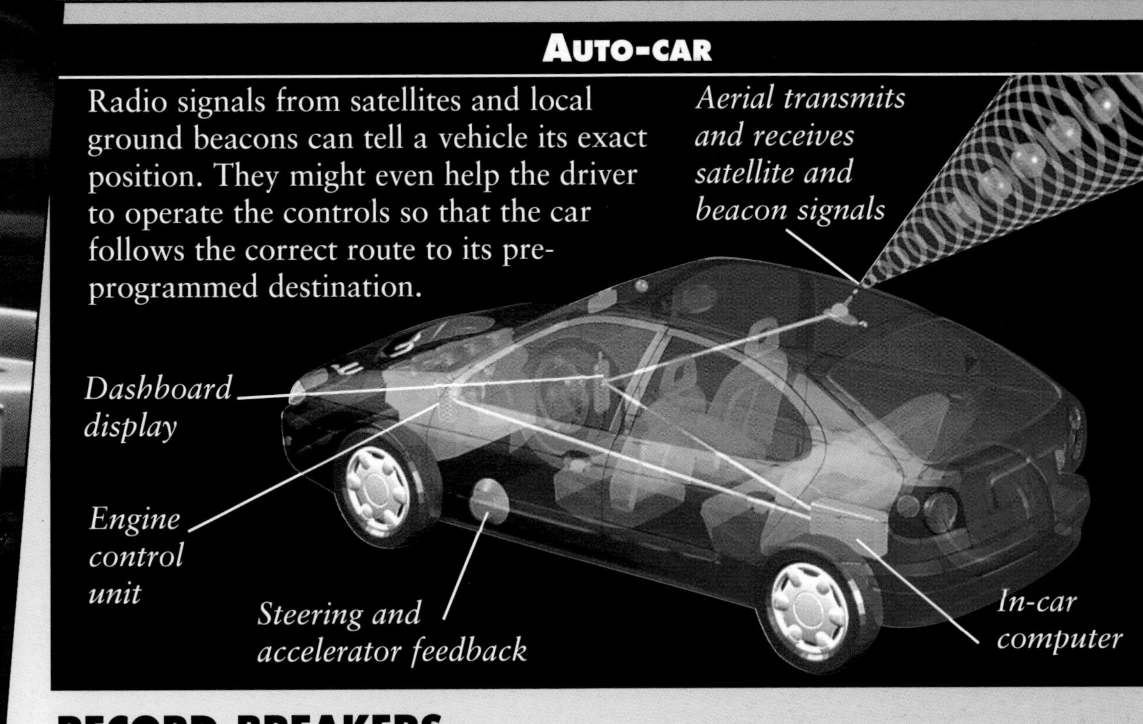


## RECORD-BREAKERS

Apart from space rockets, the most expensive craft ever built had its first flight in 1989. The first delivery to the US Air Force was in 1993. It was the Northrop B-2 Spirit 'stealth bomber', with a price tag of some $600 million. The bat-like wing design has curves, zig-zag edges, body coverings and special paint designed to make it undetectable by enemy radar. The B-2 was proposed in the late 1970s during fear of a global nuclear war between the US and USSR superpowers. The US proposed to build 132 of these aircraft. But by the late 1990s the number had fallen to about 20.

*The B-2 has a wing span of 52.4 m and a top speed of 760 km/h. It is powered by four turbofan jet engines.*

*In 1997 Andy Green drove the Thrust SSC twin-jet car to a world land speed record of 1,227 km/h. It was the first car to break the sound barrier – SSC is 'supersonic car'.*

# GREEN TRAVEL

**In the 1990s, vehicle-makers took more notice of public concerns about the environment. Their new models were 'greener' – they wasted less fuel and precious natural resources, they produced less pollution and they could be recycled more easily.**

*Modern mini-cars employ existing technologies made smaller. They use up less fuel, raw materials and road space.*

*Electric cars rely on batteries which are conveniently recharged overnight.*

Club Med 1 *is a luxury cruise ship that can use sail power to save engine fuel.*

## CONTINUING PROBLEMS

The car offers freedom to travel when and where we wish, with our luggage and passengers protected from the weather. But a car takes huge amounts of metals, plastics, other raw materials and energy to manufacture. Electric cars are kinder to the environment, with motors 90 per cent efficient compared to 30–40 per cent for a petrol or diesel engine. By the late 1990s they were at last appearing in some major cities.

## Recycling the car

An old car on a scrapheap represents a huge waste of natural resources. New guidelines in various regions state how much of a car should be made from recycled materials, especially plastics. Guidelines also state how much of the car should be recyclable, that is, which parts can be used again in the future.

*Plastic parts made from recycled materials*

*Plastic parts made to be recyclable in the future*

*The BMW 3 series*

## ALTERNATIVES

Technology can devise 'green' alternatives to the car, such as the electric bicycle and faster, more comfortable methods of public transport. But people have become very attached to the convenience and freedom of their own vehicles. It is not so much a problem for science but for society, to change people's ideas and expectations.

## COMBINED TECHNOLOGIES

Some innovative projects combine technologies from the past and present. For ships, low-tech wind power is effectively free but hi-tech engine power is reliable and convenient, so some new craft have both. The ship's computer analyzes wind speed and direction and calculates if fuel can be saved by raising the sails – and if so, how many sails and at which angles.

### FINE-WEATHER TRAVEL

The greenest, healthiest and most energy-efficient way to make short journeys is by bicycle. However in cold, wet places this is an awkward way to travel. One attempt to make cycling more attractive is the electric bicycle. Rechargeable batteries in the frame power an electric motor, with normal pedals for added push.

*The Zike electric bicycle combined electric and pedal powers.*

# GENE GENIE

**The ’90s is remembered as the decade of Gene Power. Genetic information in living things was read, engineered, modified, duplicated and patented. In 2000 came an enormous achievement – knowing all of our own human genes.**

## GENETIC FINGERPRINTS

Genes consist of very long, twisted chemicals called DNA, de-oxyribonucleic acid. Like any other chemical, DNA can be isolated, made pure and altered in the laboratory. A genetic fingerprint identifies one person’s DNA.

*1 DNA exists in all body parts, even skin flakes or blood smears*

*2 DNA cut into pieces*

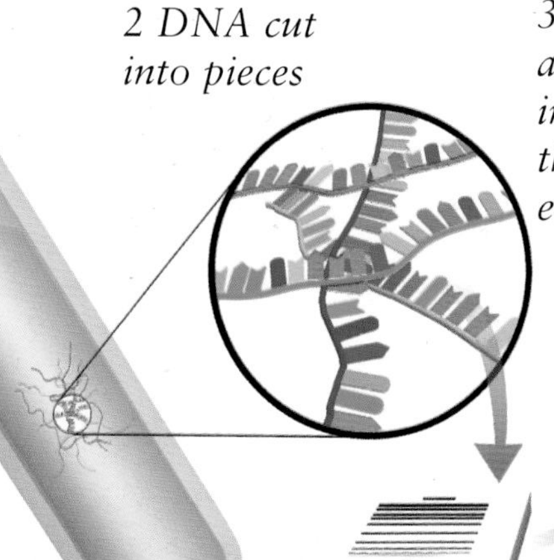

*3 DNA pieces are separated into bands by the method of electrophoresis*

*4 DNA bands are put on to a nylon sheet*

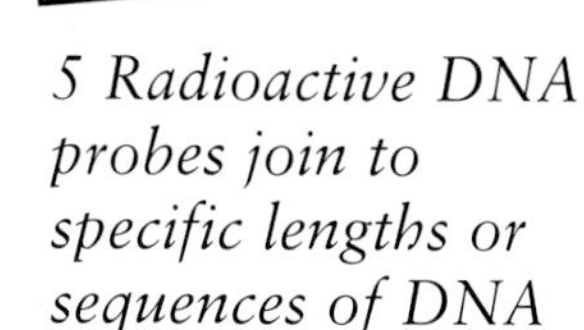

*5 Radioactive DNA probes join to specific lengths or sequences of DNA*

*6 End result is a unique DNA ‘bar code’ fingerprint*

### HUGO IS GO

The Human Genome Organization, HUGO, was set up in 1990. Its task was to unravel the 100,000-plus genes in the human genome – the complete set of instructions for developing and maintaining a human body. But the project, carried out mainly by governments and universities, encountered delays and problems. Its finish date was pushed beyond 2005. Then private genetic companies got involved, and by 2000 the ‘gene map’ was complete.

*A lab worker separates DNA samples.*

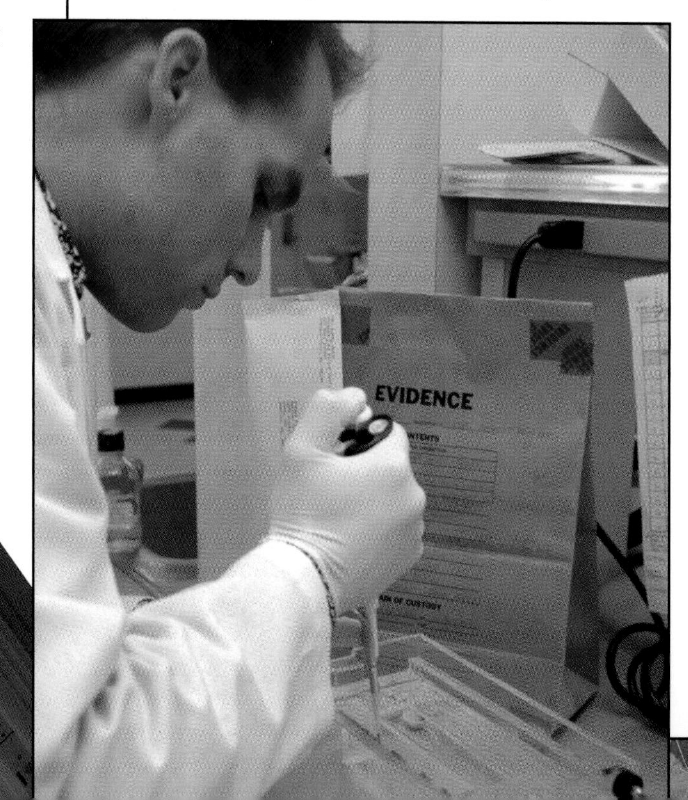


*Small dark bars indicate certain DNA sequences or codes which are parts of genes.*

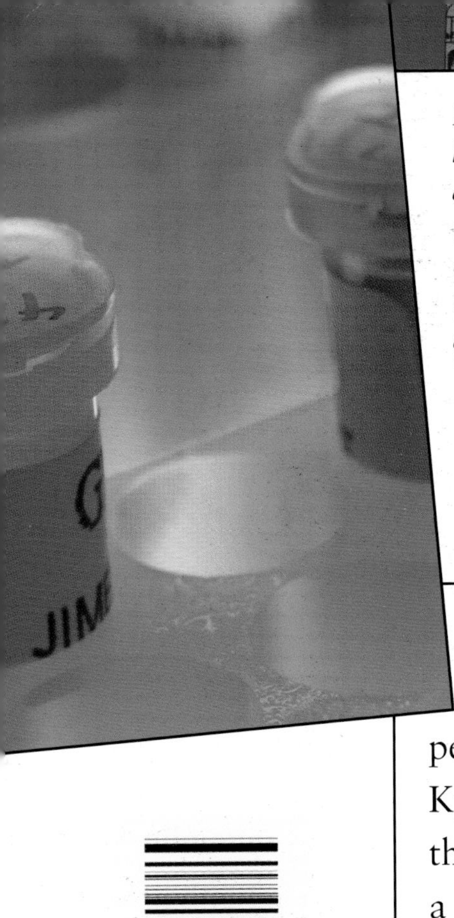

*Dolly made headlines in 1997 as the first clone (identical genetic copy) made from cells of another adult mammal.*

*The tiniest sample of a living thing can yield material to make a clone or fingerprint.*

## ULTIMATE IDENTITY CARD

Genetic fingerprints have been used since the 1980s to identify people from tiny samples of their body – even a hair or drop of saliva. Knowing the human genome is another vast step forward. It identifies the job of every main instruction or gene in the body. But there is still a huge task ahead, to find out exactly how each gene works and if it can be replaced or 'mended' to cure a genetic disease.

## THE GM DEBATE

During the '90s farm crops including maize, soya and tomatoes had genes altered or modified. For example, an added gene could protect the plant against certain weedkillers, so its fields can be sprayed more effectively. But some people worried that modified genes might swap naturally into wild plants and animals. They compared it to letting a dangerous genie out of its bottle. Once escaped into the environment, the genes can never be 'put back'.

*GM (genetically modified) crops and even farm animals could help global food shortages (above). But protesters feared genes might 'escape' and so disrupted GM crop tests (left).*

# ON THE MAKE

A '90s key word was 'smart'. Microchips programmed as tiny electronic brains could monitor and control all kinds of structures and processes, from washing machines and skyscraper elevators, to factory production lines and whole computer networks.

## THE SMART WAY

Engineers also began to use CAD, Computer Aided Design, more widely. The computer took the designer's basic ideas, filled in the details and showed how the finished product might look. It carried out complex calculations such as the breaking strain of a crane's cable or the wind resistance of a particular car body shape – all in electronic form, before any physical parts were made. This saved great amounts of time, raw materials and energy. It also made products more reliable and safer.

*Engineers and designers use CAD to compare the strength of machine parts made from materials such as metal or plastic.*

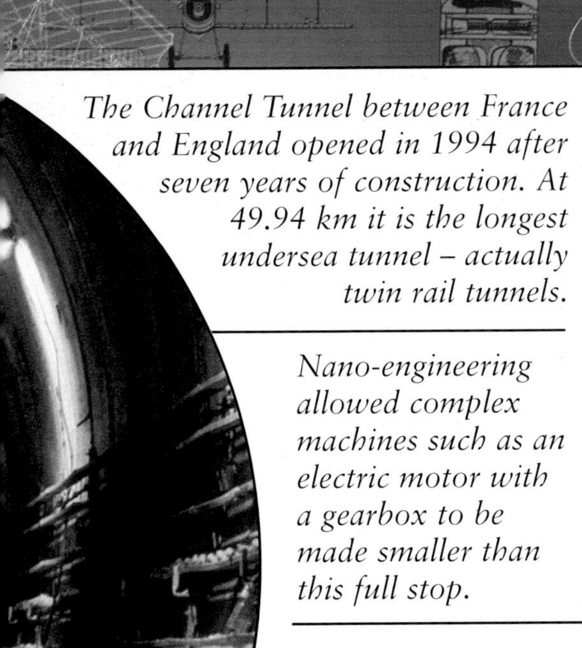

*The Channel Tunnel between France and England opened in 1994 after seven years of construction. At 49.94 km it is the longest undersea tunnel – actually twin rail tunnels.*

*Nano-engineering allowed complex machines such as an electric motor with a gearbox to be made smaller than this full stop.*

*The Petronas Towers are 451.9 m and 88 storeys tall. The 'sky bridge' link is on floor 42.*

## TIGER TECHNOLOGY

As the 1990s progressed, technical innovation occurred at an increasing rate in the fast-expanding countries of South East Asia. Their so-called 'tiger economies' and adaptable work forces attracted money from the rich Western nations, to develop all kinds of products from microchips to oil tankers. Symbols of this growth were the gleaming twin skyscrapers of the Petronas Towers in Kuala Lumpur, Malaysia. Completed in 1997 they became the world's highest building, taking the record which had been held for 22 years by the Sears Tower in Chicago, US.

*The 'tiger economies' of South East Asia provide millions of jobs in manufacturing industries, particularly electronics.*

# ELEC-TECH

**The microchip revolution continued through the 1990s as electronic parts became more powerful and faster, yet smaller and cheaper. The most widespread result was the mobile phone. In a few years this went from a bulky rarity to a small 'must-have' lifestyle accessory.**

### OLD AND NEW TECHNOLOGIES

The 'wind-up radio' was developed for use where there is no electricity supply and batteries are not readily available. It works by human muscle power. After winding up, the clockwork mechanism unwinds slowly and spins a small electricity generator which powers the electronic circuits. The radio runs for 1–2 hours on 1-2 minutes' winding. It's very successful and also eco-friendly – it does not 'waste' batteries.

*The clockwork radio and its inventor, Trevor Baylis, have won many awards.*

*With a new-generation mobile phone and laptop computer, you can link into the Internet and access almost the sum of human knowledge.*

## MORE AND MORE MOBILES

In 1997, Finland became the first country in the world to have more mobile phone numbers than ordinary 'fixed line numbers'. By 2000, more than half of the people in Britain had a mobile phone. Throughout the 1990s, the phones themselves reduced in size and weight by four-fifths. Yet they developed many new features such as 100-number phone book memories, voice-mail, text messages and advanced WAPs (wireless application protocols) to allow more types of links and also Internet access.

## OFFICE ON THE MOVE

Portable computers also became much smaller and lighter, yet faster and more powerful, throughout the decade. Several different types appeared, each specialized for certain jobs. A typical palmtop type runs for many hours on one battery charge, uses various powerful programmes from word processing to graphics, yet can be slipped into the pocket. It has a 'docking port' for connection to a larger computer (see next page), so that work carried out on the move can be transferred easily. A notebook-type computer is specialized mainly for word processing.

*Modern palmtops can perform more functions than ever before, including access to the Internet.*

### NEVER GET LOST AGAIN!

In 1994 the GPS became fully operational. The Global Positioning System is used for satellite navigation. Three groups of Navstar satellites have different orbits around Earth. The seven satellites in each group follow each other on the same endless journey. Each sends out radio messages consisting of its own identification code, its position and a very accurate time signal.

Anywhere on Earth, at least three satellites are within range of a GPS receiver. This detects their signals and compares the times they took to arrive, which shows the distance to each satellite. The system pinpoints the receiver's position to within a few metres.

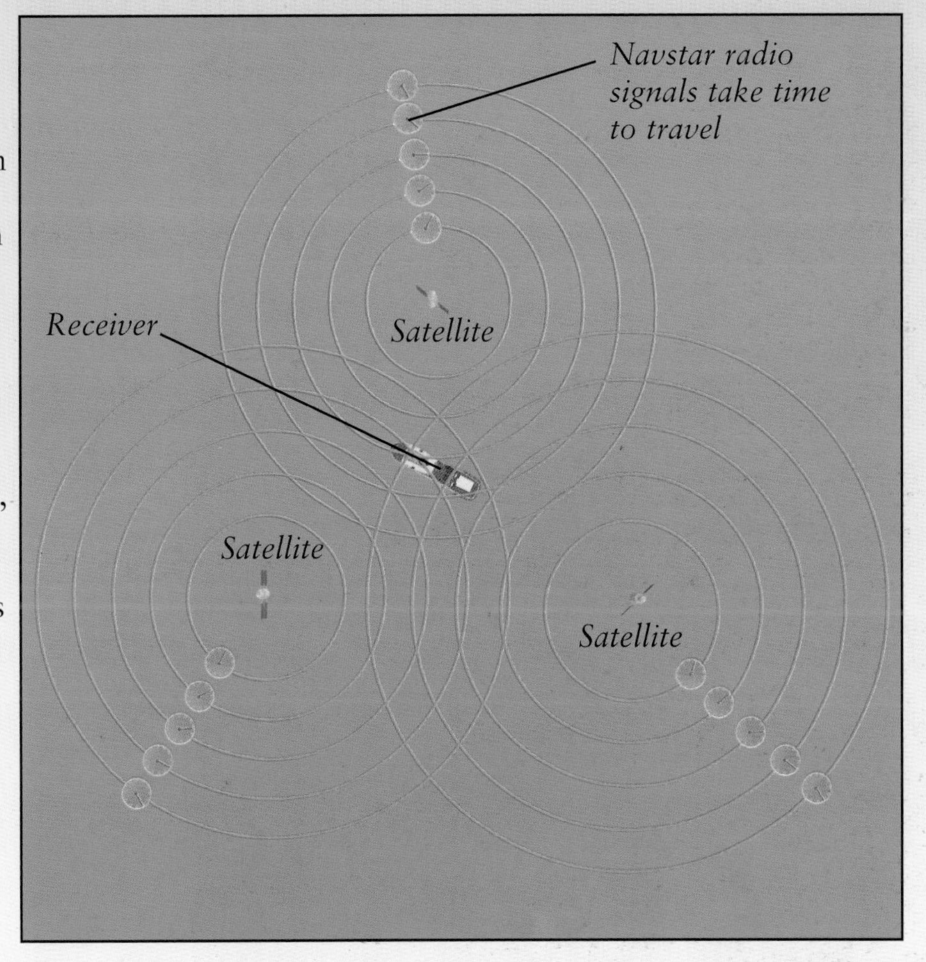


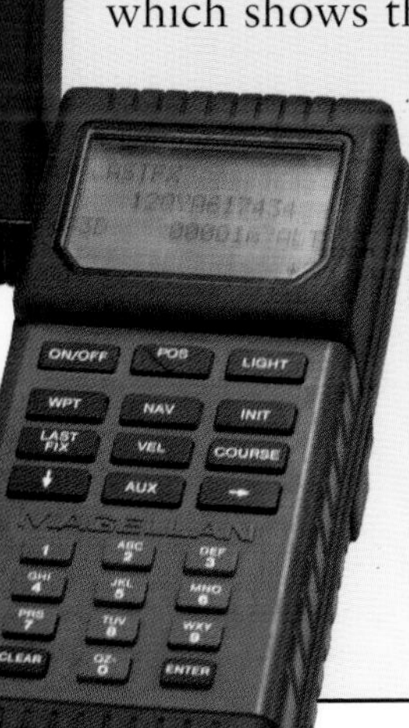


*Hand-held GPS receivers display a location using map co-ordinates or an actual map of the area on the screen.*

# ON SCREEN

**One worldwide survey estimated that between the years 1990 and 2000, the number of screens in the world increased 100 times. More and more people look, not at the real world, but at images on a screen.**

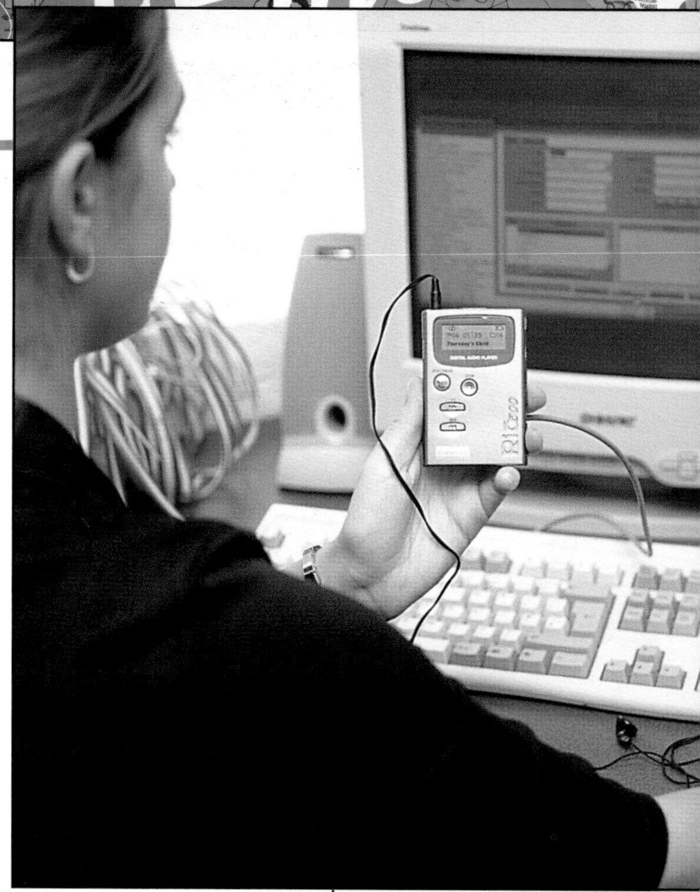

*The computer is the central unit of a growing system, as shown above right. It can be used for work or play, watching TV channels, listening to music, chatting on and surfing the Internet – and playing games.*

## SCREENS EVERYWHERE

Screens of various types are now found almost everywhere, not only on televisions and computers. They are used for video cameras, data displays such as those in control rooms and on aircraft flight decks, in camera security systems and for medical scanners in hospitals. Giant screens at stadium events allow people at the back of the crowd to have a better view.

*The video camera screen allows the user to see what has been recorded as though on a real TV, and either keep it or erase it.*

## SCREEN TECHNOLOGY

There are two basic kinds of screen technology. One is the box-like electron beam type first devised in the 1930s under the name CRT, 'cathode ray tube'. Beams of tiny particles, electrons (formerly known as cathode rays), are fired at the rear of the glass screen and make tiny dots of phosphor chemicals glow. Flat screens are much thinner and lighter and use less electricity that CRTs, but they may not be quite so bright, sharp and clear. They mostly use LCD (liquid crystal display) technology. Tiny crystal-like units can let light through or block it depending on the electrical signals they receive.

## A growing system

During the '90s more people teleworked – used a computer-based system linked by the phone lines of the telecommunication system to colleagues, e-mail systems and the Internet. This increased the numbers of people working partly or wholly from home by about five times. An increasing variety of inputs and outputs can be joined to the basic computer.

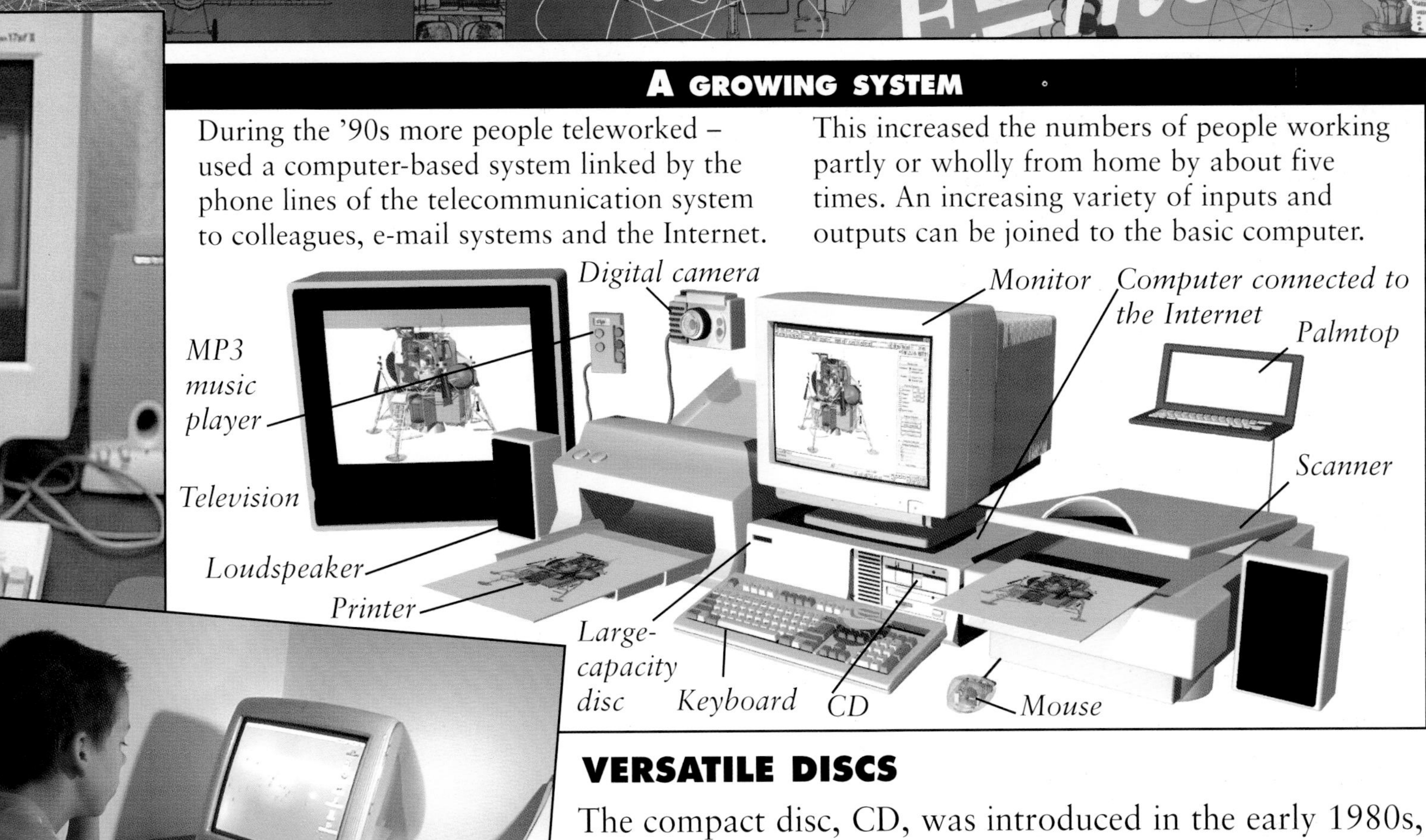


## VERSATILE DISCS

The compact disc, CD, was introduced in the early 1980s, mainly as a way of storing recorded music. However the disc is not limited to music alone. It can hold any form of information or data in the same digital format, as codes of microscopic pits in its surface which are read by a tiny laser beam. During the early 1990s more computers had CD-reading devices. They could read or obtain information from the disc, such as programmes, words, pictures and sounds. But they could not write or put information on to the disc. They were called CD-ROMs (read-only memory).

*Apple's iMac range of computers did not come with removable discs as standard. Information was meant to be fed in and out along wires.*

In the mid 1990s more computers had CD-writers or 'burners' to put data on the disc (see page 25). The DVD, digital versatile disc, is similar to a CD but can hold up to eight times the amount of data.

*A DVD can hold enough information, and read it quickly enough, to show a whole full-length movie with hi-fi soundtrack.*

# DIGITS AND DISCS

**The computer, Internet and micro-electronic revolution of the 1990s was based on digital technology. What does 'digital' mean?**

## TWO NUMBERS

Digits are single numbers such as 1, 2 and 3. Digital systems change information into codes that use numbers. Most common is the binary digital system which has just two numbers, 0 and 1. In electronic devices such as a computer or CD player these correspond to a pulse of electricity (1) or no pulse (0). Any information including sounds, pictures, words and mathematical calculations can be changed into this coded form, as long strings of 0s and 1s. This is called digitizing the data.

*The MiniDisc system is designed to record or store information on to the disc, as well as reading or obtaining it from the disc (see opposite).*

*Solid-state memory systems hold information in binary digital code inside microchips housed in 'sticks'. There are no moving parts to go wrong or wear out.*

## FLAWLESS COPIES

Digital data can be copied and read (changed back into its original form) perfectly. The copy system simply creates a new 0 for each original 0 and a new 1 for each original 1. In the alternative analogue system, information is coded by varying strengths of signals, forming wave-like shapes. When copying these, slight errors can creep in concerning the exact height or shape of the wave. So copies of copies of analogue information, such as music on magnetic tape, gradually become altered.

## RECORD AND PLAYBACK

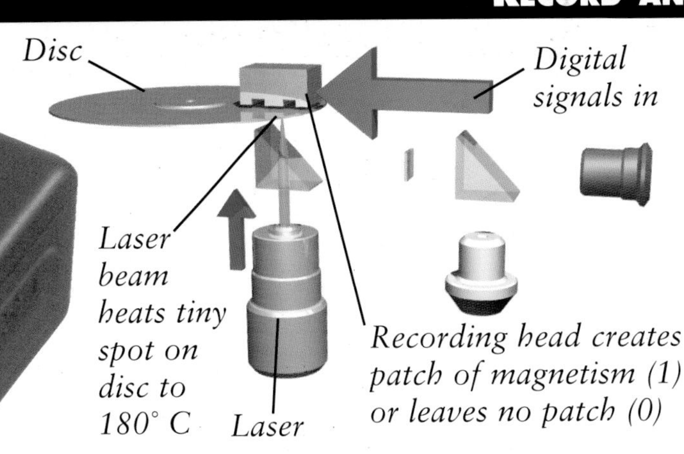


RECORDING (*writing data*)

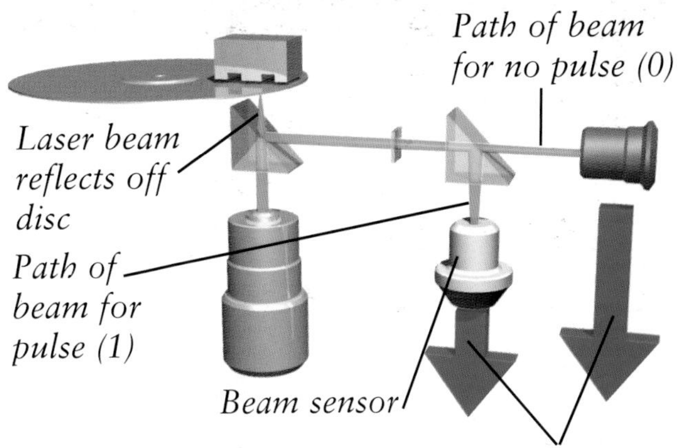


PLAYING (*reading data*)

Sony's MiniDisc system ('92) uses two different technologies to make its small compact discs re-recordable – different information can be put on to the same disc time and again. A laser beam heats a tiny patch of the metal foil on the disc. Then a magnetic recording head swipes past it to leave a tiny patch of magnetism. The magnetism is enough to alter a beam of laser light shone on to it, which is detected as a 1 of digital information. No patch is a 0.

## PERSONAL TV

The first small, portable 'pocket TVs' appeared in the 1960s. But a major problem is that the detection of television signals changes as the user moves about, so picture and sound may fade.

Modern tuning circuits can get around this problem in areas where the TV signals are strong.

More reliable is the small, portable, bright-screen DVD-TV which uses DVDs (see page 23).

*In 'TV specs' a tiny projector shines images on to the inside of the eye screen. But you can still see through it.*

*The 'personal cinema' plays movies and other programmes stored on CD-sized DVDs, digital versatile discs.*

# GAMES GALORE

**The shrinking size and falling cost of microchips and other electronic devices created a whole new area of fun and leisure – the hand-held e-game console. A plug-in cartridge contained the software or program, and a small screen showed the action.**

## BIGGER AND BETTER

At the start of the '90s, the arcade 'video games' (those based on a TV screen), in boxes bigger than a person, showed fast-moving, life-like racing cars, aliens and other typical game scenes. By the end of the '90s, such speed and quality, or even better, was available from a console as small as your hand. Some consoles plug into the screen of a TV set or computer monitor, others are self-contained with their own visual displays.

*Nintendo's Game Boy, launched in 1989, continued to be hugely popular. Colour screens and bright new cases kept it looking up-to-date.*

## LOOKING GOOD

Almost as important as what a games console could do, was how it looked. Fashions came and went, from cool greys and metallic sheens in the early 1990s to bright, brash, plastic colours and see-through casings a few years later.

*The Sony PlayStation arrived in 1995. It is said that, in its small box, is almost as much computing power as was used for the first Apollo Moon landing mission in 1969.*

Home VR systems may be the next big advance in the area of e-games. But some experts say that they may encourage certain users to retreat away from real life into an isolated virtual world.

## THE NEXT CHALLENGE

In the late 1990s some games manufacturers began to tackle mass-market virtual reality, MMVR. To produce bright, detailed images and clear sounds that change at the same speed as in real life, requires great computing power (see page 6). By the year 2000 microchips and other components were cheap yet powerful enough for some MMVR systems to go on sale. However there was much debate about their safety. Inside the VR headset, absorbed in computer-generated sights and sounds, the user is almost 'cut off' from the real world. He or she may not be able to respond to a real-life emergency.

## NEW IDEAS

The e-game craze of the '90s was the virtual pet, a small electronic device that responded like a real-life pet. It had to be fed, watered, cleaned, exercised and trained. It fell ill or even died if its owner did not take good care. Some people said that virtual pets were good training for real ones.

Virtual pets, known by the general name of Tamagotchi, were developed in Japan. They provide fun and react like real pets, for the wishful pet-owner who may not have enough space or facilities for an actual animal.

# MEDICINE

Medical science left the 20th century with more implantable parts, surgical equipment, lasers, scanners and other hi-tech equipment than ever before. People have never been healthier or lived longer.

## HI-TECH HUMAN

Prostheses or implants can replace most body parts. Some are 'false' non-working versions but electronic eyes and ears are being developed.

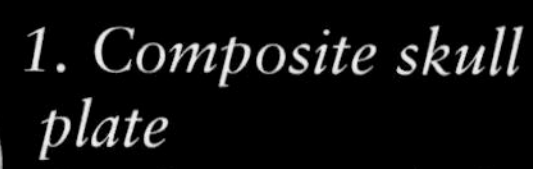

1. *Composite skull plate*
2. *Electronic light-sensitive eye*
3. *Nose bridge*
4. *Implanted hearing aid*
5. *Alloy jaw plate*
6. *Plastic chin implant*
7. *Electronic voicebox*
8. *Shoulder joint*
9. *Artificial heart*
10. *Elbow hinge*
11. *Arm prosthesis*
12. *Metal forearm plate*
13. *Replacement wrist bones*
14. *Thumb-wrist link*
15. *Ball-and socket hip joint*
16. *Thigh bone implant*
17. *Knee bridge*
18. *Artificial leg*
19. *False big toe*



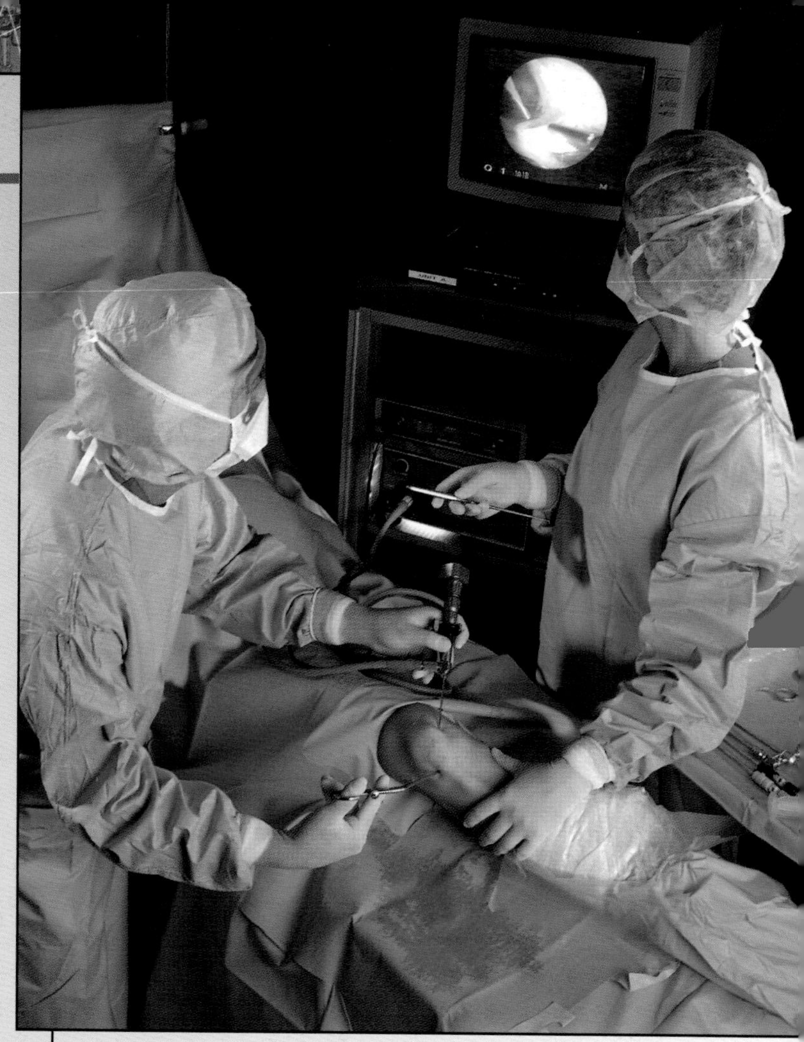

*Many types of flexible 'scopes', using bendy optical fibres, look into the living body. Here an arthroscope reveals the inside of the knee joint, often affected by sports injuries.*

## LONG-TERM BATTLES

Smoking tobacco has long been associated with various forms of cancer, also heart and lung diseases and many other illnesses. The body can become dependent on the drug nicotine in tobacco smoke. As an alternative, special patches supply nicotine through the skin. They avoid the tremendous harm caused by tobacco smoke and can gradually be reduced in strength.

*Nicotine patches supply the body with the drug it wants, without damaging the lungs.*

## MENDING GENES

Unravelling the full set of human genes (see page 16) opens up incredible possibilities for medicine. Faulty genes cause many hundreds of diseases and medical conditions. It may be possible to 'mend' them at an early stage of life by replacing the faulty gene with the correct version, known as gene therapy (right).

*Tiny samples of body tissues can be examined in the laboratory for genetic problems that may only cause trouble later in life.*

### GENE THERAPY

Viruses are the smallest living things and many cause diseases. But some can be helpful. They are used as 'carriers' to take a correct gene into a human cell. The new gene replaces the faulty one, and the human cell then multiplies to cure the condition.

*Virus genetic material snipped*

*Virus enters body cell where new gene joins human genetic material*

*Replacement gene*

*New gene is spliced into virus genes*

## THE FUTURE

During the 20th century, science and technology have achieved amazing advances, from heart transplants and high-yield farm crops to space travel and virtual reality. Yet as the 21st century dawns, millions of people around the world are still homeless, suffering and starving. A more difficult problem is ensuring that scientific achievements are used wisely, safely and for the benefit of all.

*Vaccination (immunization) to protect the body against infectious diseases, here against polio in Ethiopia, has been one of medicine's greatest-ever successes.*

# GLOSSARY

**ATOM** The smallest part of a pure substance (chemical element) that can exist naturally. Most atoms are made of three types of even tinier particles called protons, neutrons and electrons.

**CD** Compact disc, a memory device consisting of a plastic disc with microscopic pits which code for digital information such as sounds, pictures, words, computer programmes and data.

**DVD** Digital versatile disc, a type of memory device similar to a compact disc (above) but which holds more information.

**GENE** A code or instruction, in the form of the chemical DNA (genetic material), for building or maintaining part of a living thing. The human body has 100,000-plus genes.

**GPS** Global Positioning System or 'satellite navigation'. The network of orbiting satellites and other equipment that allows a GPS receiver to locate its position to within a few metres anywhere on Earth.

**LASER** A device that produces waves of intense, powerful, high-energy, pure-colour light. The term stands for Light Amplification by Stimulated Emission of Radiation.

**METEORITE** A small, usually rocky or metallic object in space that eventually falls to the surface of a planet, moon or other large body.

**PALMTOP** A computer or similar device small enough to fit into the hand.

**STEALTH TECHNOLOGY** Materials and devices that make a craft or vehicle less detectable to an enemy, especially to their infra-red heat sensors and their microwave and radar systems.

**SUBNET** A network of computers and similar devices with one or a few controlled access points. It can be a small, private network, or a sub-unit of the general global Internet.

**VIRTUAL REALITY** When something seems real to our bodily senses and brain, but is created by a computer and so is not real.

**WORMHOLE** A possible 'tunnel' through space and time, which could connect two regions such as black holes and allow instant travel over incredible distance – even through time.

**WORLD EVENTS**

- *Iraq invades Kuwait, Gulf War begins*
- *Nelson Mandela freed in South Africa*
- *USSR, former Soviet Union, breaks up*
- *Civil wars lessen in Ethiopia, El Salvador*
- *Famine and war devastate Somalia*
- *Bill Clinton elected President of US*
- *War and atrocities in Bosnia-Hercegovina*
- *Palestinians and Israelis agree peace*
- *South Africa: Nelson Mandela is president*
- *Civil war and genocide in Rwanda*
- *Earthquake destroys city of Kobe, Japan*
- *169 die in terrorist bomb, Oklahoma City*
- *BSE 'mad cow disease' beef ban headlines*
- *Taliban Muslims seize power in Afghanistan*
- *China takes over Hong Kong from Britain*
- *Princess Diana killed in car crash in Paris*
- *The euro unit of currency begins*
- *Former Yugoslavia: peace almost breaks out*
- *India and Pakistan dispute nuclear tests*
- *Russia tries to subdue Chechnya rebellion*

# TIMELINE

| | SCIENCE EVENTS | TECHNOLOGY | FAMOUS SCIENTISTS | INVENTIONS |
|---|---|---|---|---|
| 0 | •*Hubble Space telescope launched*<br>•*Geneva: World Climate Conference* | •*Rail speed record by French TGV, 515 km/h*<br>•*IBM writes its name using just 35 atoms* | •*Michael Irwin discovers a tenth small galaxy orbiting our own galaxy, the Milky Way* | •*'Toddler Tag' electronic radio bracelet for children*<br>•*First International Robot Olympics, Strathclyde* |
| 1 | •*Suggestions that 'hot dark matter', giving out infra-red radiation, may hold the Universe together* | •*Pen-sensing electronic notepads developed, to go on sale in 1993* | •*Richard Ernst's Nobel Prize for improvements to medical MR (magnetic resonance) scanners* | •*Dyson bag-less vacuum cleaner cleans up market*<br>•*Pocket electronic encyclopedia* |
| 2 | •*'Last Chance' Earth summit, Rio de Janeiro*<br>•*COBE satellite detects 'echoes of the Big Bang'* | •*Chris Boardman rides new-concept Lotus Superbike to gold in Barcelona Olympics* | •*Galileo (died 1642) receives a formal apology from the Pope that Earth does indeed orbit the Sun* | •*Renault Zoom folding electric car*<br>•*Laser potato peeler (£450,000) vapourizes skin* |
| 3 | •*Comet Shoemaker-Levy torn apart by Jupiter's gravity* | •*Movie special effects reach new heights with Stephen Spielberg's* Jurassic Park | •*Joseph Taylor and Russell Hulse receive Nobel Prize for discovery of binary or twinned pulsars* | •*Video phones*<br>•*Truth phone (voice stress analyzer is designed to detect untruths)* |
| 4 | •*Genes linked to breast cancer are identified*<br>•*Number of Internet users breaks 30 million* | •*Aircar (Sky Technology), a roadworthy car that can take off as it speeds up* | •*Philip Gurner invents the laser-guided pea-shooter for World Pea-Shooting Championships* | •*Flavr Savr genetically modified tomatoes*<br>•*Zeta strap-on electrical power pack for bicycles* |
| 5 | •*Satellites show the Antarctica ice cap is shrinking by 1.4 per cent every 10 years* | •*'Liquid bone' Norian SRS can be injected to stabilize a break and gradually changes to real bone* | •*Harold Cohen of San Diego writes a computer program, Aaron, that develops its own art style* | •*Trevor Baylis's Freeplay wind-up radio*<br>•*Vidicall videos callers and the time they arrived* |
| 6 | •*Possible microbe fossils in meteorite from Mars*<br>•*Internet reaches 50 million users* | •*Physicists at CERN European centre make first anti-matter, anti-hydrogen (but only nine atoms)* | •*Smalley, Curl and Kroto receive Nobel Prize for golfball-like 'buckyball' molecules* | •*Sony PlayStation computer games system*<br>•*Benecol cholesterol-lowering margarine* |
| 7 | •*Adult mammal cloned, Dolly the Sheep*<br>•*World's oldest rocks: 4,000 million years* | •*Dutch scientists use a very strong magnet to make a frog float or levitate in mid air* | •*World chess champion Gary Kasparov beaten by IBM Deep Blue 2 computer program* | •*Wind-up torch and more clockwork gadgets*<br>•*Lawn-nibbler fully automatic lawn mower* |
| 8 | •*Construction of International Space Station begins* | •*Best-selling VW 'Beetle' car is given a hi-tech make-over for the new millennium* | •*US surgeon Denton Cooley (over 45,000 open heart operations) receives National Medal of Technology* | •*Apple iMac range of computers*<br>•*DVD compact discs become widely available* |
| 9 | •*A new artificial chemical element, number 114, is created* | •*Japan builds largest single telescope mirror, 8.3 m across, in Hawaii* | •*Ahmed Zewail receives Nobel Prize for taking billion-billionth-second photos of molecules* | •*Smart city car*<br>•*DreamCast computer games system* |

# INDEX